Mobile Security: A Guide for Users

David Rogers

About the Author

David Rogers

David Rogers is a mobile phone security expert who runs Copper Horse Solutions Limited, a software development and security company based in Windsor, UK. Alongside running the company, he also teaches the Mobile Systems Security course at Oxford University. David's articles and comments on mobile security topics have been regularly covered by the media worldwide including The Guardian, The Wall Street Journal and Sophos' Naked Security blog. He judged for the 2012 and 2013 Global Mobile Awards at Mobile World Congress in Barcelona.

Formerly he helped to establish the Wholesale Applications Community (WAC) which aimed to give developers a one-stop shop to many manufacturers and app stores through HTML5 and widget technology. He served as Chairman of the Security Group and Head of Security until February 2011. He has worked in the mobile and semiconductor industries for over 18 years in software engineering and security.

David has advised government departments and international law enforcement agencies on a number of mobile phone theft, security and forensic issues. He continues to champion the pioneering work in the mobile phone industry on embedded security within handsets. This work has led to widespread adoption of hardware security to protect security-sensitive applications such as m-payments.

David holds an MSc in Software Engineering from the University of Oxford and a HND in Mechatronics from the University of Teesside.

He blogs from: http://blog.mobilephonesecurity.org and tweets @drogersuk.

The Copper Horse website is at: http://www.copperhorse.co.uk.

Contents

1   Introduction

Mobile devices touch all of our lives in more ways than we can possibly imagine. They get us from A to B and record our day-to-day life through imagery, location updates and messages. Through applications and the web they give us access to tools which help us do our jobs and generally make life easier; they can even let us pay for things.

More and more parts of our lives are being integrated to mobile and some people predict that they'll entirely replace cash before too long. Device functionality has developed at an incredible rate and the sheer array of technology integrated into both handsets and tablets now is bewildering for most people to even start thinking about how to deal with all the security aspects.

Security is a difficult and wide-ranging topic and has sometimes been described as more of an art rather than a science. With humans involved at both ends of the scale from user through to attacker, anything can happen and frequently it does.

This short book explains the types of attacks that could take place on mobile devices such as handsets and tablets and how users can defend and protect themselves against such issues. It was originally written for the Police in the UK and they kindly suggested that we make it available more widely. There are basic guidelines contained within which will help users to prevent and minimise technical security incidents, as well as practical security advice on using phones while out and about. The book also discusses some of the upcoming technologies in 2013 and onwards that might not be known about, but all of which come with new types of security considerations for us all. One of the most difficult tasks when it comes to mobile security is keeping ahead of the threat in such a fast paced technological environment. There is little doubt that multiple new and evolved attacks will be made public after publication, but this book provides a snapshot in time and some core principles which will remain relevant.

2   The History of Mobile Security

Mobile phones have evolved at an astonishing rate, so it is sometimes good to step back and understand how we got here. This section explains some of the history and key evolutions in mobile security.

There have been people wanting to break into the security of wired and wireless communications for one reason or another, almost from the very start of the technology. As far back as the 1850s during the time when the Wheatstone telegraph was used as a means of communicating on the railways in Britain, the railway companies needed to introduce encryption and separated lines of communication to counter security issues.

When Marconi demonstrated his 'secure' wireless telegraph to the Royal Society in 1903, his demonstration was disrupted by magician John Nevile Maskelyne who broadcast the word "rats" repeatedly over the morse code link, in order to prove that the wireless telegraph was actually insecure. At the time, it was described as "scientific hooliganism". Fast forward to today and such attacks would probably be described as "cyber hacktivism".

In the 1920s, in-car Police radios were introduced to Detroit. Journalists were amongst the people keen to listen in to these messages so that they could get their next story. In the UK, the Wireless Telegraphy Act of 1949 outlawed this practice by making it illegal to disclose any information overheard on radios. Encryption on Police radios was not to be introduced to the UK until the 2000s.

In the military world, wireless communications were introduced and widely used in the Second World War. For obvious reasons there has always been a need to keep such radio messages secure. The most famous story of all is the breaking of the German Enigma encryption system by Bletchley Park which helped the Allies to win the war.

In the 1960s, cellular technology was invented by Bell Labs, using towers to relay signals in hexagonal cells, based on original concepts which had been created for Police radio cars in the 1940s. This is sometimes referred to as 0G and was fairly limited (the user had to stay in the same cell). In the late 60s, the first portable Police radios were introduced to the UK and by 1971, the first cell phone service was introduced by AT&T in the USA.

Fixed line telephone hacking and tampering was known as "phone phreaking", which was popular in the 1960s and 70s. The "Blue box" was a piece of kit that generated tones which allowed for free long distance calling. A couple of the most famous pranksters were Apple's Steve Jobs and Steve Wozniak! Pranksters later used "Orange boxes" and other types of hacking kit for spoofing caller identity and other types of fraud. These boxes evolved into software in the 1990s. Many of the same individuals involved in these communities became involved in the emerging computer hacking scene.

The first 'mobile' phone call was made by Motorola in 1973 and it took until 1980 before the first portable cellular phone was put on sale to the public: the Motorola DynaTAC 8000x. The AMPS system (Advanced Mobile Phone Service) which was an analogue mobile network system was used in the USA from 1982 through until the 1990s, in some countries only finally being turned off in 2007. The UK used TACS (Total Access Communications System) and this was introduced to customers in 1985. Vodafone eventually turned off their ETACs network in the UK in 2001.

Analogue systems were dogged by poor security – a lack of air-interface encryption allowed people with the right equipment to easily eavesdrop on conversations, whilst the telephone numbers of devices were programmed into insecure chips on handsets. This was attacked by fraudsters who were able to change numbers of phones, clone legitimate ones and even 'tumble' calls so that they could use a different number for each phone call. The networks tried to address this by performing velocity checking (i.e. checking that a call made in Los Angeles wasn't immediately followed by a call in New York), but it wasn't really until the introduction of a secure token called the SIM card in GSM that these problems could be properly solved.

In 1982 the "Groupe Spécial Mobile" committee was formed which would eventually lead to the development of the GSM that we know and still use today. By 1987 the GSM Memorandum of Understanding was signed which led to the creation of the organisation that now represents over 800 mobile networks in the world, the GSM Association. By 1991 the first GSM call was made by Nokia in Finland and the first ever SMS message was sent in the UK the following year.

Mobile phone handsets were still pretty basic until the 21st century, but mobile phones still had features that criminals and hackers were interested in. Network operators had created a "SIM lock" which would ensure that they could sell devices for low prices to users, but keep the handset on their network for a fixed amount of time. This artificial manipulation of the device's true value created a massive grey and black market for getting these cheap devices unlocked and into countries where they could be sold at full price. Users themselves were incentivised to unlock their phones as operators would often make it difficult for them to do it legitimately and people didn't know the true value of the technology in a lot of cases. Market stalls were soon offering "unlocking", which used hacking tools which were often developed in Russia, Eastern Europe and China. In addition these tools would have other functions, such as being able to change the device's identity – its IMEI number which could have been blacklisted by a mobile phone operator if the device was stolen. Manufacturers were beginning to be drawn into an underground security arms race against embedded systems hackers which continues even to this day. Mobile operators also had to start dealing with different types of call fraud, spam and premium rate scams which they still continue to have to address.

A UK company, Symbian Ltd was formed in 1998 which would see the creation of the first widely popular "smartphones" where third-party applications could be installed.

In 2001, the UK government identified that there had been a large rise in the number of phones being stolen. This led to the creation of the "Mobile Phone (Re-Programming) Act in 2002" and the "National Mobile Phone Crime Unit" which still exists today. In fact, the original figures were flawed and hadn't taken into account peculiarities around insurance claims that led to people reporting lost phones as stolen. It was clear though, that as mobile phones became more and more popular that criminals would be interested in them too. The industry worked closely together with the UK government and created its own set of rules for network operators blacklisting devices to improve, and for manufacturers making devices who agreed upon nine technical security principles for device security.

In 2002, Research in Motion's Blackberry really took off with its first GSM device being shipped. The following year they would get security certifications which would allow them to sell into government. The same year sees the first camera phones being launched including Panasonic's GD87.

In 2004, the first mobile malware issues occurred, mainly basic proof-of-concept malicious applications targeted against the Symbian operating system which was installed on a lot of Nokia devices. It was clear that some of the technology was entirely new to hacking groups and with a tiny proportion of the mobile market being one breed of smartphone, the chances of widespread mayhem were minimal. In the same year, there were some widely publicised hacks on Bluetooth due to a security flaw deep inside the code used by a number of manufacturers. One type of attack, "Bluesnarfing" was demonstrated by security researcher Adam Laurie outside the House of Lords where he was able to extract the phonebooks of some very important people. Both sets of problems were manageable for the industry but served as a wake-up call that new technologies bring new challenges and new types of attack. Shortly after, a piece of malware was created which has probably become the most costly to the industry: "commwarrior". This could self-replicate to the entire phonebook of a user and mainly spread as an MMS attachment. Even this problem was miniscule compared to the number of devices and users in the world, who were increasingly starting to use smartphones.

Various other types of security issues came and went, often theoretical issues or bugs that could be quickly dealt with. The world's first commercial spyware emerged in the form of an application called "FlexiSpy". One of the GSM air-interface encryption algorithms which protects call confidentiality (A5/2) was thoroughly proven as broken and withdrawn by the industry, but the stronger A5/1 held firm despite having been designed in the 1980s with limited key lengths and having to endure repeated attacks by researchers such as the German Karsten Nohl.

In the latter part of the decade, the industry was given a good shake-up by the launch of the iPhone in 2007 and Android in 2008. It was time for smartphones to really become smart. Apple had chosen to go for a much more locked down approach towards applications that could be developed and approved every single application before it would appear in the app store. Google's Android took the opposite approach. They were much more open towards development in order to encourage innovation.

The design of the security architecture of Apple's devices was reasonable but they lacked experience in the industry. Hackers from the SIMlock hacking world helped a 17 year old called George Hotz to jailbreak the first iPhone spawning a whole new industry and non-approved apps to be installed on the device. Google's business choice allowed malicious innovation too, but they didn't suffer too badly due to technical measures they'd taken to eradicate malware and the increasingly widespread ability across industry to fix security bugs by updating software over-the-air or via USB cable. The openness of Android enabled the anti-virus industry to try and break into mobile, which resulted in the Android ecosystem being tarred as completely insecure (which in actual fact was far from the truth).

Building on the work of the 9 principles a few years earlier, the industry published new recommendations for hardware security through the industry forum OMTP. The Trusted Environment: TR0 and the Advanced Trusted Environment: TR1 (which was endorsed by the UK Home Secretary) set a new benchmark for mobile device hardware security leading into the future, in preparation for security-requiring business models like mobile banking and to harden devices against emerging types of hardware attacks. This work continues now in the industry forum GlobalPlatform as well as in the GSM Association Security Group.

By the turn of the decade, hacking groups and criminals were really turning to smartphones, attracted by the popularity amongst users of the two major platforms Android and Apple. Attacks have happened against all sorts of parts of the mobile ecosystem – taking advantage of users connecting to Facebook over insecure WiFi in cafes, creating malicious QR codes for users to scan, through to applications which extract the user's data from their devices. Newer types of network equipment were also being targeted by researchers, such as mobile network femtocells used as range extenders. The first major organised criminal tools against banking were also being converted over to include mobile too with the launch of the mobile malware ZitMo.

In 2011 the News of the World "phone hacking" scandal erupted with thousands of potential victims. It appeared as though getting access to people's voicemail was a routine tabloid technique for getting stories. The actual attack that had been used to get to voicemails was not really hacking – it was a combination of social engineering and using default

PINs through remote access numbers – both of which shouldn't have been in place and were a result of poor security design and control by network operators. On the industry side, this resulted in the publication of security guidelines by the GSM Association soon after the scandal broke. UK network operators quickly took measures to increase the security of voicemail systems and users were warned not to setup PINs on their accounts and to avoid the use of obvious PINs.

During the 1990s and into the early 2000s, there were still some major competing types of telecommunications networks between Europe, the US and places like Japan. Eventually GSM and 3G won over to become the dominant global communications system that we now use. The next generation networks called LTE (Long Term Evolution) or 4G are already being rolled out which will enable much higher-speed data and improved security. At each stage of development, new security has been introduced to combat attacks against previous systems. General advances in technology also allows for much more sophisticated monitoring and detection systems.

By 2013, security had significantly evolved but so had the hacking techniques. Nobody in the 1920s could have possibly thought that mobile phone applications would now exist to listen into unencrypted Police radio messages around the world via the web. New technology is being developed that will make us even more connected, via the cars we drive, the homes we live in and the way we look after our health. Good security and maintaining that is now more critical than ever.

3 Keeping Safe when using a Mobile Device: Personal Safety Aspects

Mobile devices can both add to personal security and become an issue for personal security. The simple fact that you're using an expensive phone in a "dodgy area" can make you a target, but it is also the item that could be your lifeline in an emergency. Most people use their phones without a second thought for what is going on around them. People are so tied to their online lives now that that they need to be constantly connected, even to the point where some people have walked into lamp posts or straight out in front of cars because they've been so busy texting or updating Facebook.

It is important that people have a certain level of situational awareness when they're using their phones.

3.1 Walking, Driving and Texting

3.1.1 Walking

It seems so obvious, but a lot of us have turned into "texting zombies", walking around engrossed in our mobile phones, busy updating Facebook and Twitter whilst completely oblivious to the world around us. A recent survey by Safe Kids Worldwide showed a significant increase in teenage pedestrian injuries and fatalities attributable to using phones and music players whilst walking[1]. In Brick Lane, London, lamp posts were even covered in padding to protect people from walking into them whilst texting, becoming Britain's first "Safe Text" street!

3.1.2 Driving

Mobile phone use whilst driving is illegal in the UK, yet driving and texting is a big problem. RAC Foundation research has shown that reaction times are reduced by 35% by young people when reading and writing texts[2]. The report also said that around 50% of young drivers texted while driving. The simple fact is nothing is so urgent that you should run the risk of an accident whilst using your phone at the wheel.

3.2 Susceptibility to Personal Attack

Situational awareness is reduced drastically by being distracted whilst using a mobile phone. This means that you are personally vulnerable to attack from someone who wants to steal your phone, or worse. In fact a potential attacker is more likely to target you because you're obviously not paying attention to your surroundings.

A lot of people like to listen to their music whilst out running or walking on their own, especially in remote areas. Another thing that women often do is talk to their partners on the phone while walking home late at night, in order to feel safe. The logic behind this for most people is that if anything happens, at least the partner would hear straight away and would be able to react and that an attacker would be put-off by there being a potential witness. However, in both cases the awareness aspect is the most important so at least you will have a good chance of sensing if someone is coming up behind you. Remember also, that if you're using the phone at night, the phone is going to be lit up brightly like a beacon, which in itself is going to attract potentially unwanted attention. This applies also to the volume of the ringer: discreetly turn your phone to vibrate or silent mode if you feel unsafe.

3.2.1 What you can do

If you can avoid running with your music on, this is probably the best option, but keep your phone in a safe place on your person so that if you do find yourself needing to call for help you can do. If you're being followed and suspect that the person has ill-intentions other than wanting to steal your phone, pretending you are on your phone may be a better strategy than actually making a call to a loved-one, as you're still able to keep your senses active to what is going around you, however it is generally inadvisable to have the phone out. An attacker may try and smash a phone (in fact these days, if someone is going to attack you, they probably expect that you're going to have a phone on you anyway), but there is no point in making it easy for them by having it in your hand.

Another option is to download a personal safety application. PanicGuard is one example[3] which is also recommended to victims of domestic violence. These applications can help people with their confidence and can do a variety of things such as alert your emergency contacts, record video and audio and activate a loud alarm. They are quite sophisticated so that if for example, you stray from a pre-programmed route, this would be enough to activate the safety features.

The Suzy Lamplugh Trust also provides a list of specific "Lone Worker Devices" on their website[4].

Finally, if someone does snatch your phone, let them take it. It is not worth getting into a fight with someone who may be under the influence of drugs or who could be armed with a knife. More information on mobile phone theft is covered in the next section.

3.3   Personal Safety Guidelines:

*   Don't use your mobile phone while driving – it is illegal and nothing is so urgent to cause an accident.

*   Be extra careful when walking around texting or listening to music on your phone, your senses are impaired and you could run the risk of something worse than a bruised ego for walking into a lamp post.

*   Keep your senses about you – don't unnecessarily listen to your music or use your phone if you feel unsafe, especially at night where the bright lights of the phone will draw attention.

*   Discreetly turn down the ringer volume on your phone to vibrate or silent if you feel unsafe to avoid inadvertently drawing attention to yourself.

*   Consider downloading a personal safety application if you feel at risk of personal attack.

*   If someone snatches your phone, let them take it. Don't increase your personal risk by putting up a fight.

4 Lost and Stolen Devices: What to Do

No matter who you are, there is a risk that you could lose your phone or have it stolen. It is important that you take all measures to ensure that as a user, you are prepared for that eventuality. This will ensure easy recovery, more peace-of-mind when it comes to data security and potentially a thief that gets caught.

Smartphone theft seems to be on the increase again and this is probably down to both economic factors and also technical reasons. Smartphones are becoming easier to re-use by thieves in some ways, partly because users don't secure them with PINs and keylocks and partly because stolen phone blocking is being avoided by criminals. This is achieved either by exporting stolen devices (blocking only works in the home country in most places), or by just not using the features of the phone which were blocked – the telephony. The thief can continue to use all the other features but just over WiFi. Calls and messaging can still carry on, just using over-the-top applications like Skype or WhatsApp. All the most attractive features of the phone: the games, music and web functions will still work. This is a real problem that needs to be addressed by industry and governments worldwide.

4.1 Physically Protecting Your Phone

Thieves are often opportunistic, so keeping your phone out-of-reach and not visible is extremely important. If you're sat in a café or bar, don't leave your phone on the table. It is a prime target for snatching or a distraction theft. Of course, make sure that any handbags or rucksacks are secured too; trapping a chair leg around a handle is a good way to prevent a bag being stolen. One common method for distraction theft is to push a tourist map in front of you whilst an accomplice steals your phone from the table.

Keep your phone in a front pocket or zipped up in a bag, never in the back pocket of your jeans. Remember not to leave the bag itself unattended. Phones are often stolen from handbags in nightclubs when people leave them to go on the dance floor. Crowded environments such as this also give good cover for thieves. Pickpockets often target rock concerts and gigs and come away with large hauls of mobile phones.

Don't leave your phone or tablet on display in your car or on the side of the sofa at home where thieves can see it through the window. Always take valuables with you from your car. Don't be tempted to hide things away in the boot as a thief may be sitting watching you and will know exactly where you've put them. For valuable items at home, put them out of sight of windows.

4.2   Be Aware of Your Surroundings

Phones are an attractive target to thieves and whilst they're with us all the time, they can be snatched or stolen easily. Think about your surroundings when you're about to use your phone. Do you really want to turn your phone on, just as you walk out of the tube, or can you do it further down the street? Also consider your personal safety, as discussed in the last section.

Have you ever been walking along and browsing on your phone such that you haven't noticed that someone's near you? You are particularly vulnerable if you're tied up doing something else. You're also at high risk from theft if you're in a crowd of people. Your phone can be snatched very easily and the thief can also get away easily before you can identify them. Snatch thefts are high in cities like London, particularly in crowded tourist and shopping areas like London's Oxford Street. Try and keep your hands in your pockets if you can, protecting valuable items such as your phone and keep any bags close to you and well protected.

Places of vulnerability will include areas where there are obvious network black spots - for example the exits of an underground station. The first thing most people do is get their phone out and check it. Thieves are often waiting to take advantage of this.

Think carefully about where you are. Are you in a high crime or dangerous area? If you are, you need to adapt your behaviour accordingly. If you're somewhere strange and you're busy on Google Maps trying to find out where you are, this is probably as bad as standing there with a tourist map of the area!

Be aware that criminals can be very discerning. If you have the latest brand new expensive smartphone, this is going to much more attractive to thieves than a really old phone.

4.3   Take Technical Steps to Protect Information

Once your phone is stolen, it could end up anywhere. The security measures that you take to protect your phone have to be relative to the type of data you are protecting. If it is very sensitive business information, there is a chance that the data could get to someone who shouldn't have it, so the device needs to be protected appropriately. In the vast majority of cases, devices are stolen for their intrinsic value rather than someone being specifically targeted, but you need to consider your own security needs.

Technical measures are discussed later in this document, but using a PIN lock is one of the best ways to stop a thief from getting access to your data and re-using your device.

4.4   Always Backup Your Data

This is something that is always on the to-do list but never quite gets done. Take a little time to think about what would happen if you lost your phone and phone numbers and how it would affect you. Then think about what you can do to mitigate that. There are lots of services and tools out there to help you do this on a regular basis without thinking about it. Choose one you trust, or if you decide to backup your data yourself, make sure you do it regularly and store it in more than one place just in case your backup fails. Just remember though, that if you use a "cloud" service, all of your data is going across the internet and that could be sensitive or private information, so be careful which method you use.

4.5   Record Your Phone's Identity Number

The International Mobile Equipment Identity (IMEI) is what identifies your phone to the network and is located on the back of your phone underneath the battery. Another way to get your IMEI number is to type *#06# into your phone keypad to display it. When you get your new phone, it should be also on the side of the box. Keep the box label in a drawer just in case you need it. If your phone is lost, report the IMEI number to your service provider and they can block your phone so it can't be used to make calls. If it is stolen, you should also give the IMEI number to the Police.

You can also register your phone's details and IMEI number on the UK National Property Register at: http://www.immobilise.com/. This helps the Police to return lost or stolen property to its correct owner and to identify if a criminal is carrying a stolen phone.

4.6   Learn How to Remotely Lock and Wipe Your Phone

Losing your phone or having it stolen does happen and when it does, what do you do to prevent someone getting access to your work or personal data? This is where lock and wipe services come in. Many handsets now support applications which you can use to stop someone getting access to your data and if you're sure you can't recover it, to delete your data. These services can give you invaluable peace of mind if the worst happens. Some services can even help you locate your lost phone by using the GPS function of the device to work out where it is. Some devices have this functionality in-built, for example on Blackberries. The Samsung Galaxy SIII has the "Find my mobile" feature using SamsungDive fully integrated, but the user still needs to remember to set it up. Another example is the "Find My iPhone" service[5]:

Other mobile security suites (which often are created by anti-virus companies) also contain this kind of functionality. Because they are third-party applications they may be susceptible to being wiped if a criminal resets the device. Examples of these types of apps include Lookout Mobile Security[6]:

One of the downsides is that criminals react to technology too. Recently, thieves have begun to realise that they can be tracked. One of the first things they do after stealing a smartphone is perform a complete system reset or to completely turn off the GPS functions until they can get rid of the device. This makes locking the device with PINs all the more important as they wouldn't be able to get access to do this. On the iPhone, setting a Restrictions passcode for Location Services will ensure thieves cannot disable 'Find My iPhone'. This situation is what happened to Channel 4 journalist Ben Cohan. He wrote an article explaining to people how they can secure their iPhone location settings entitled 'Dial M for mugging'[7].

4.7   Minimise Critical Data on your Device

Think about what data is actually on your phone or tablet – is there anything that is on there that probably shouldn't be or is unnecessary? Have you stored a banking PIN in your phonebook or hidden passwords in notes on your device? Even if you have put lots of security on there, it's probably best to keep any work and personal information to a minimum. This gives you more peace-of-mind if you do lose your device and ultimately could reduce your risk of further security issues.

4.7.1   Lost and stolen devices guidelines:

- Keep your phone out of sight where possible. Don't leave your phone out on a café table where it can easily be snatched.

- Keep your phone in a front pocket where it is safer, never in the back-pocket of your trousers.

- If you keep your phone in a bag, make sure the bag is zipped up or secured and that the bag itself isn't left unattended or easily stolen.

- Think carefully about whether the area you're in is safe. Don't use your phone at obvious places for theft such as the exits to tube stations.

- Try to minimise any personal information or business critical or sensitive information you store on your device.

- Don't store PINs and passwords on your device insecurely.

- Backup your phone's data on a regular basis, but be careful about using "cloud" services for sensitive information.

- Learn how to remotely lock and wipe your device. Some devices have this in-built. If you need to get an application to do it, download it now rather than regret not doing it later.

- Use your device's PIN lock to prevent thieves getting access to data on your device.

- On the iPhone, setting a Restrictions passcode for Location Services will ensure thieves cannot disable 'Find My iPhone'.

5   Technical Threat Vectors

Mobile phone technology is advancing every day. It is difficult for security professionals to stay on top of all the potential security issues, never mind normal users! This section outlines some of the main technical vectors via which an attacker can get access to a mobile phone. There are many different motives for someone to want to attack your phone. Often it is not specific to you as an individual, but just occasionally these attacks can be specifically targeted, particularly for people in more sensitive professions such as the Police.

How does malware actually get onto a device and how can a device be attacked? There are multiple ways that an attacker can get to your device. Think about all the interfaces on your phone, physical and virtual. Any one or a combination of these could be used as a way in to conduct various types of attack. Potential attack points could be:

- the USB / charging connector
- microphone
- dialer
- applications
- email
- the browser / websites
- device access control and remote management features
- voicemail
- SMS
- WiFi connection
- Bluetooth
- camera / QR codes
- Near Field Communication (NFC)
- cloud services

If an attacker has physical access to your device, many security professionals would say that "all bets are off". This is because many different avenues for attack are opened up. However, if you look closely at the problem, there are things you can do to mitigate the ability for someone to manipulate your device whether to install something or to remove something. Different attackers have different objectives. Probably the most likely attack against a device that is not in the hands of the user is the "jealous spouse". This attack is extremely common; the attacker has considerable access and also the intent to do it. This is discussed in more detail later.

5.1   Click-jacking via Social Media Sites

Social engineering you to do something you didn't want to do or expect is one of the ways that an attacker can achieve his or her goals. In fact an element of social engineering is involved in the majority of successful attacks today. A reasonably recent trend is to lead a user to a rigged website that can then do something nasty, exploiting flaws within the web browser or even in the way an application handles data. We have all seen friends who've clicked on something by mistake on Facebook or Twitter and who've then spammed all their friends with the same type of attack. This can be a nuisance at best, but could potentially be really damaging. Often the victim has no clue what they're clicking on and they're lured in by either a message directed at them personally (possibly from someone they know and trust) or by the promise of a funny link or video.

Don't be lured into clicking on an unknown link to a web page. A phone's screen is much smaller and it is often more difficult to see a full link to a website and verify that it is what it says it is. Not only this, but links are often shortened so you can't actually read the proper website it goes to. If you get messages or posts on Facebook and Twitter with links, stop and think. Do you know the sender? If you do, is this something that they would send you? If you do click, it is often too late once you realise that there is a problem. Don't react or reply to spam messages you may get over SMS or Bluetooth.

5.2   Premium Rate Scams and Fraud

There are many different types of scams involving premium rate messaging and calling, some of which are covered in other sections of this book as they can come in from a variety of sources.

Fraudsters have turned towards mobile applications as an attractive way to make money, however it is true that there are easier ways to commit fraud and make much more money using traditional telecoms fraud methods which target the telecoms operators rather than those which hit individual users.

There are still scams that exist such as encouraging people to dial premium rate numbers in advertisements or things like 'wangiri' which is 'one ring' fraud – enough to put a missed call on a phone, but not enough to make it actually ring out to be answered. The user is then tricked into ringing a premium rate number as they'll probably try and call back.

Mobile network operators do a lot in the UK to try and break down these frauds but keeping strong control of premium rate short codes for SMS does seem to be a problem for them. This is probably because of the amount of resellers and often companies using the same short-code through an aggregator.

5.2.1   Spam

The most common source of phone-related spam is over SMS. Sometimes the spammers can get your number from buying marketing lists or from you putting your number on the web. Be careful who you hand over your mobile number to and think about whether it is necessary to include it on forms you fill out or competitions you enter. Sometimes, speculate spam texts are sent out such as those which advertised injury claims "claim up to £3000 for your recent accident" or for claiming money on mis-sold payment protection insurance. The spammers were making their money by selling on 'positive hits' to solicitors. Some of these spammers are based outside of the UK in places like India. In November 2012, Tetrus Telecoms was fined £440,000 by the Information Commissioners Office for spamming mobile customers with texts[8].

For SMS in the UK, users can report spam to the following short-codes:

- O2, and EE: 7726
- Vodafone: 87726
- Three: 37726

If you are concerned you should also call the customer services department of the operator to report the issue and get numbers blocked.

Never reply to spam messages, they may cause you to be charged at a premium rate. Often unscrupulous premium-rate providers will sign you up for more messages which you'll get charged for. Despite the introduction of the "STOP" command that is supposed to prevent any further messages being sent by premium rate services, this in itself has been abused and shows to the spammer that they've got a live number. Always check your bill for anything unusual. Complaints can be launched with PhonePayPlus at: http://www.phonepayplus.org.uk/.

5.3 Counterfeit Devices

The market for counterfeit mobile devices is huge and difficult to control. It is not unique to the mobile industry – many other types of goods are counterfeited and eventually sold in the UK. As with most other fakes, these devices are of a much lower quality than the original product. Reports of "exploding phones" are usually caused by users using counterfeit batteries bought for a very low price. Due to the lack of the correct protection circuits, the batteries overheat and sometimes burst, presenting a real safety risk. In addition there are unseen risks – the radio performance is likely to be very poor and the phone transmitting at all the wrong power levels; the increase in radiation is potentially harmful. Users also don't know what they're getting in terms of the software on the device. It is likely to be pirated and low quality, but it could even be pre-installed with malware.

These products are often sold overseas. There are varying estimates that between 30-50% of the phones in Uganda are counterfeit[9]. Some countries in Africa have resorted to turning off all these devices, based on the IMEI number of the phone – but these IMEIs are often taken from legitimate manufacturers' number ranges which are publicly available on the internet, so it can be difficult to truly detect them. With deliberate attempts to fool users into thinking the device is the real thing, at first glance, the device may seem to be the real thing – as is shown in an advert for the "Blockberry" device, alongside a picture of President Barack Obama![10]. Some things to look out for in counterfeits are unusual features such as in-built TV, multiple SIM support or the 'wrong' operating system. For example, in the "Blockberry" advert, there is a Windows Mobile logo – real Blackberries run RIM's own Blackberry OS. Ultimately it is a case of "buyer beware". If something is much cheaper than it should be, it probably isn't legitimate.

5.4   QR Codes

QR codes are the most popular form of 2D barcodes around and have become extremely popular in the marketing world. Users scan the barcode using an application on their phone which utilises the phone's camera.

The barcodes are mainly being used for easily communicating web links to people so they can quickly get access to a long web-link without having to type it in. They can also be used to dial numbers and send messages.

QR codes have only become really popular in 2011 because of the rise in the number of smartphone users and the increasing popularity and usability of the mobile web. A variety of applications are available to read QR codes and in some handsets this functionality is pre-installed. From a security perspective, QR codes represent a risk. The user often has no view at all of what the QR code links through to, which could easily be something malicious. A lot of companies have rushed into implementing this functionality for making things more convenient for people without thinking about security properly.

One example of a poor and insecure implementation of QR codes was the Verrus paybyphone parking service[11] which encouraged people to scan a QR code to pay for their parking quickly over the web. The QR code took users straight to a mobile site which asks users to enter their credit card details. The site is so astonishingly easy to spoof that it is scary, partly because screen space is so confined that the user can't see the whole of the URL (which might actually lead to a malicious site instead of the real Verrus one). An attacker could easily stick a replacement QR code over the top of the original code on the parking sign, taking the user to their malicious payment site instead. There was no description whatsoever near the sign's QR code about what it was supposed to do. There were a whole host of other attacks that could potentially take place too.

There are a number of threats to mobile users from the misuse of QR codes. Here's some of the types of attacks that can take place and the terminology used:

- QRjacking – This is the practice of putting stickers over existing QR codes which link to wherever the attacker wants them to go.[12]

- Scanjacking (as opposed to clickjacking) – Demonstrations have shown that malicious code could theoretically be inserted into QR codes as a 'payload' which causes the device to do something the attacker wants.[13],[14]

- Man-in-the-middle attack – This is where again a sticker is placed over the legitimate QR code or is falsely advertised in a newspaper or magazine. The user has their credentials captured or bank details taken, then they are redirected back to the correct website with an error such as 'you didn't type your details correctly'. It is unlikely that the average user would pick up on what was going on.

- Phishing – Randomly posting QR codes that entice people to scan them but actually go to something malicious is highly tempting for attackers. An attacker could probably even get people to attach to their fake WiFi network. It is not difficult to imagine lots of places that could be targeted e.g. bars, bus stops etc. This could of course happen via email, asking a user to scan and download an application to their phone.

- Spear Phishing – Extending the Phishing method described above, but targeting a particular individual or a small group (imagine dropping a fake competition flyer around an extremely upscale bar).

- Premium rate SMS fraud – One of the things that is supported with QR codes is the ability to make calls and send SMSs. It would be trivial to perform a premium rate fraud using fliers for a competition at a concert or sporting event. Less so for call fraud because of the time and hassle involved for the user, but depending on the social engineering aspects of the attack, it could be done.

- Pre-registration fraud – There was one incident where Nokia had failed to register a short link (bit.ly) on a QR code (the link just led to nowhere) which could have quickly been hijacked by an opportunist[15], this would probably be technically classed as a pre-registration fraud although very rare.

- False Advertising – This is a sophisticated attack on a company, perhaps by an activist group by putting fake QR codes in advertisements. It is obviously incumbent on magazines and newspapers to check adverts and their sources anyway, but this is probably not done in a lot of cases. Even if some form of checking did take place, it could be side-stepped by only putting the malicious content live once the target publication is in the shops.

In practice the 'real' risk to users is actually reasonably low. The preparation needed to execute an attack and the fact that physical things need to be done (such as printing and sticking labels over real signs), mean that such attacks are rarely seen in the 'wild'. Other attacks rely on socially engineering the user into taking an action themselves. The risk is still there though and users should always check the URL of a code they've scanned. Some of the better barcode scanners will automatically show users where the link leads to before actually taking the user there, even translating shortened web links to the real destination. They then require the user to confirm that this is where they want to go.

5.5   Near Field Communication (NFC)

Near Field Communication (NFC) has very similar functionality to QR codes although instead of needing to a scan a code the phone's camera, the phone is equipped with a tag reader which uses radio frequency at close range to read data from tags. The tags are embedded in everything from posters through to door entry cards. NFC has much more functionality than QR codes, enabling it to be used for ticketing and payments.

Many of the attacks described in the previous section are exactly the same for NFC. The tag provides convenience for the user – it can quickly take the user to a web link, dial a number or send an SMS. The only difference in many cases for the bad guy is that sticking a replacement NFC tag over an existing one requires the attacker to put foil underneath the replacement sticker to block the signal getting through from the original tag. German researcher Colin Mulliner demonstrated many of these attacks in 2008[16] when extremely few devices were available, but many of the attacks remain valid. Today, NFC is becoming a standard feature on devices although many users are probably unaware it is there.

Something that it is unique in the NFC world is the brush-past attack. With many NFC enabled credit cards and transportation cards out there, it is theoretically possible with an ordinary mobile phone to be able to read credit card numbers or other information from any NFC device within proximity. This attack has been demonstrated on news programmes across the world: an attacker stands very close to his victim in a lift and extracts their credit card details from their NFC enabled card. In practice this is extremely difficult as anyone who has tried to read a device through a bag or wallet will know. As the technology is increasingly adopted, users are likely to also have multiple NFC-enabled cards in their wallets which can cause conflicts – further hampering an attacker. Unless the film crews and demonstrators were extremely lucky, the demonstrations of this kind of attack have been rigged. It is however likely that future attacks will attempt to read NFC devices at long-range, which will represent a greater risk. At a hacking conference in 2012, the famed iOS hacker Charlie Miller demonstrated an interesting hack which used NFC to completely takeover a mobile device and extract data from it. This forced fixes to be issued for some Android and Nokia devices. The demonstration showed that NFC attacks could do much more than just get a credit card number from a card when combined with other security breaches.

Widespread adoption of NFC mobile payments has not happened yet using mobile devices. There are various reasons for this but a form of "touch payment" is likely to be the way that most people will be paying for things in the future. The attractiveness of this feature to all sorts of criminals will mean that there will be a thriving market for exploiting vulnerabilities and issues with the underlying technology. At the moment, mobile network operators' marketing departments want NFC to be turned on in devices by default (which is not a secure-by-design method) to encourage adoption of the technology. They don't want any barriers to user uptake. When NFC is activated on a mobile device, it is usually displayed as a small 'N'. It can be turned off like any other wireless feature in the settings menu. Some companies are starting to sell 'shielded' wallets which are lined with a metal mesh or foil to create a Faraday cage effect. This may or may not become a standard feature of purses and wallets (it works for some passports which contain the same type of chips) but is unlikely to be useful for phones – the Faraday cage will also block phone calls getting through!

5.6 QR and NFC Guidelines

- Get a good QR code reader – one that allows you to review a link after you've scanned it and lets you choose whether or not to complete an action.

- Be extremely careful, alert and wary when scanning a QR code or NFC tag, don't just scan anything assuming it'll be ok.

- Don't allow a QR code or NFC tag to dial a number or send an SMS unless you are absolutely sure you know that the number is legitimate. Otherwise you may end up with a very large phone bill.

- If it looks too good to be true, it often is. If you're handed a flyer or competition with a QR code enticing you into some fantastic offer, think about whether it is legitimate or not – is it trying to just get your personal data or worse, trying to lure you into a security trap? A simple Google search is often enough to reveal scams.

- Check to see if the QR code or NFC tag is physically the original if scanning a poster. Someone may have placed a sticker over the top of the original code or tag to try and get you to download some malware or give away your details.

- Don't give away information needlessly – if a site asks you to connect to Facebook or your bank, does it really need this? Remember you can always close the site and walk away. You do not have to enter your details and it is not recommended that you do.

- Always check a web link to be sure it is going where you expected it to. Check the address bar at the top of the page. Is the website unusual? Have you been redirected to another site? If the barcode scanner software on your phone has shown you the link for the website, is it the same?

- Turn off the NFC feature if you aren't using it – it is better to be safe by default.

5.6.1 Attacks from the web and through NFC and QR – an example

In September 2012, a researcher called Ravi Borgaonkar revealed that he could wipe the Samsung Galaxy SIII phone just by it visiting a rigged website or through the user scanning a rogue QR code or scanning an NFC tag. This potentially was one of the worst issues to hit the mobile industry in a very long time.

The way the attack worked was to abuse the ability to dial telephone numbers by using a web resource. A rigged website could make the browser execute "tel:" (and then a number), then the phone would automatically put this number into the dialler and dial it. The mistake was that it didn't allow the user to confirm the number that was being dialled. The attack exploited special codes that the manufacturer had created in-house. Some of these codes are standardised – for example *#06# is a well-known code that displays the identity (the IMEI) of the device. The special code that was abused in this case would reset and wipe the entire device. It is incredible to think that such a destructive function was available in this way. As this was only Samsung's code, it looked as though other devices weren't affected. However this was not the case and in fact the way that the "tel:" codes were handled was much deeper within the Android operating system. The researcher had 'responsibly disclosed' the issues to Samsung and various operators (as well as some other manufacturers), but got frustrated by a lack of response or action by some of them, so he decided to go public with the issue. This could be perceived as an extremely irresponsible move on his part given the potential of this issue, but is a not uncommon action by security researchers who don't necessarily see the whole picture.

In addition, the researcher had not realised that leaving special codes aside, if a website could easily dial a number with no user-interaction, why not a premium rate number? What about other codes – for example talking to the SIM card?

The combination of an easy-to-repeat attack, the fact that some devices were vulnerable because they hadn't been updated and the ease of executing another type of attack that the researcher hadn't thought through were potent. The complexity of the mobile supply chain and the difficulty with which software updates can be pushed out to all devices was a stark warning that had this been a really malicious attack, millions of users across the world would have been very severely impacted.

5.7 Voicemail Security

Voicemail security was brought into sharp focus in 2011 with the News of the World "phone hacking" scandal. This wasn't in fact phone hacking, but illicit and illegal access to voicemail in order to intercept the messages of celebrities and many other people in the public eye, including Police officers and the families of victims of terrorism. It appeared that such practices had been going on in the media and private investigations world for some time.

The main issue revolved around a security flaw in the voicemail systems of mobile network operators. Someone could dial the "remote" number of a voicemail account, use a publicly known, common default PIN number and then listen into the messages. Users would have no clue that their voicemails would have been listened to, apart from some new messages would be marked as 'old'. Since then, further security measures have been put in place so that users will get a text message notifying them if attempts have been made to get into their voicemail account. It still remains the case though that you can continue to use your voicemail without any PIN at all.

Newer techniques exist for listening into voicemails, but can be protected against by using a PIN number. The usual precautions should apply to your voicemail PIN security (e.g. not using the same PIN as bank accounts, not using dates of birth and not using obvious PINs such as 1234).

5.8 Device Access Control

There are different ways to control access to your device, from a simple swipe to unlock, through to biometrics such as fingerprint control (discussed in a later section). Controlling access to your device is critical for your security.

5.8.1   Gestures and patterns

Some manufacturers provide gesture control for access using pattern recognition on touch-screen devices. Users tend to go for less complex patterns and this has led to attacks where people can see the grease marks on the screen and get into the device, so-called "smudge attacks". If you have to use gestures, as a rule of thumb, use gestures that overlap back on themselves.

5.8.2   PINs and passwords

PINs and passwords can be a pain as they but a barrier in the way of things you do repeatedly. These days it can be difficult to remember all your different PINs and passwords or be very tempting to use the same password for everything. Make use of the handset locks to protect your data and messages. With touch-screen phones, these are often gesture based, meaning that a convenient swipe is all that is needed to unlock your phone, whilst still keeping your phone safe.

If you choose to use a password, don't use words from the dictionary as there are tools out there that can perform dictionary attacks against certain types of access control and badly stored passwords. It seems pretty obvious, but people still do it – don't write passwords down. If you really need to keep a copy of your password, make sure it is locked away somewhere very safe.

Learn how to manage your passwords without having to remember lots of complex details. You can do this by using password management tools which can store lots of different passwords and generate random ones for you. Make sure these are also backed up in a safe place. Remember that some of these services will store the encrypted data on their servers, rather than you having it locally – this can be convenient, but you're still relying on the company you're giving it to doing their job correctly. One example of such a service is LastPass[17].

One thing is certain, if you don't have proper access control to lock your device, you are putting yourself at a high risk of the device being abused, either from casual access by another person or from much worse if your phone is stolen.

5.9 Device Access and Purchasing Guidelines:

- If you're using a pattern to access your device, don't use gestures that can easily be identified by the grease marks on your screen.

- Make sure you setup a PIN for your voicemail.

- Get into a security habit by enabling the user PIN on your device and using it.

  o Don't use easily guessable PINs such as 0000, 1234, dates of birth etc. and keep it secret.

- Don't use words from the dictionary for passwords.

- Change your PINs and passwords at regular intervals.

- Don't reply to spam SMS messages, even with STOP. You'll probably get charged or receive even more spam.

- Be careful which websites and companies you give your mobile number.

- Always check your phone bill for unusual charges.

- Don't buy or use a counterfeit phone or battery – it may be unsafe and the phone could even contain malware.

- Don't buy phones over the web from auction sites or from other people. You can't be certain that the device itself hasn't been pre-installed with malware, even if it seems new. Always buy devices from an authorised retailer.

5.10 Data-at-Rest Attacks

As discussed in other parts of this document, if an attacker has sufficient physical access to your device, then they will probably be able to do something bad, whether it be installing Spyware on there or removing all the data. Some manufacturers take this very seriously. RIM for example can securely wipe the data from a device if it has not been accessed for a set period and other manufacturers are starting to provide remote wiping features. Being able to remotely lock the keypad prevents casual access, but a determined attacker equipped with forensic software may be able to get around this. In the most extreme circumstances, if your data is stored 'in the clear', i.e. it is not encrypted, it may be possible for an attacker to get access to all the data that was on the device. This certainly falls into the 'unlikely' category for the vast majority of users, but as data becomes increasingly valuable and more credentials for online services, social networking and email are stored on devices, the value of extracting this data also goes up. Even recycling a device can be a risk if the recycler does not have a proper data deletion process. There have also been a number of embarrassing examples where customers have received 'refurbished' handsets from their phone company only to find that someone else's data is stored on there still. As a user, consideration has to be given to the balance of convenience of access, how valuable the data is and what would happen if the data falls into the wrong hands. Third party tools also exist that allow users to protect or scramble data using encryption.

5.11 The Threat from the Network

Users have a lot of confidence in the security of mobile networks but rarely think about it. Since the introduction of WiFi on devices, users have multiple choices that can be made in terms of how to access the internet and not all of them are secure.

5.11.1 WiFi

The most risky method of accessing the internet is over an open WiFi connection in an internet café. Users frequently do this because a) it is free! and b) it is easy and convenient. Because nothing ever happens, this has become defacto behaviour for users, however the threat is mostly unseen. The costs of international roaming on mobile networks means that normal users have almost no choice if they want to connect to the internet other than to use the free WiFi in a café or hotel. There aren't really any definitive figures on the numbers of compromised open hotspots out there but there are lots of stories of people who've entered credit card details into a 'cheap' WiFi service at an airport or who have logged onto sensitive services such as online banking, webmail or social networking services.

The perpetrators usually need nothing more than a laptop to set up a cloned or fake hotspot, but can often takeover and compromise open WiFi routers in cafes, bars and libraries, especially if no encryption exists at all on the WiFi network as anyone can 'sniff' the traffic.

The services themselves have often been to blame for not providing enough user security. Huge providers such as Google, Facebook and

Twitter have all been forced to improve their provision of SSL protected connections (ensuring that your connection to a website is confidentiality protected and can't be easily seen) and also to improve the way they authorise people to connect to sites. The theft of authentication cookies by tools such as Firesheep[18] was ridiculously easy and these companies did not act responsibly in terms of the security of their users. Many of these problems have now been addressed in the big sites, but problems still exists and new attacks are always being developed.

One measure that users can take is to use a Virtual Private Network (VPN). This means that your internet connection can go through a secure 'tunnel' which either you control or a trusted third party controls. Traditionally these have been really difficult to setup and quality of the connections could be described as 'flaky'. Symantec recently released the Norton Hotspot Privacy[19] - this is an example of an easier way of setting up a VPN connection that can be used across multiple devices and it doesn't cost too much for the peace of mind it gives.

5.11.2   The mobile network

The mobile network family (GSM, GPRS, UMTS (3G)) are usually owned and operated by the mobile network operators (in the UK, Vodafone, EE, O2 and Three). Some other companies operate services on top of these networks as 'virtual' operators (for example Virgin Mobile). The companies who operate the networks have a lot of obligations that come with the license they get from the government to operate the network. The operator is also incentivised to protect the user from attack by the fact that they will lose revenue themselves through fraud and loss of confidence by users. Traditionally what is known as the 'macro' network has been physically protected – e.g. fences and security around base stations and other network equipment, but this is starting to change. The introduction of 'small cells' has led to some people having mobile network access points (called Femtocells) in their own homes in areas of poor coverage. Companies are starting to own parts of the network infrastructure in order to provide mobile coverage to employees inside buildings or shopping centres. Hackers are starting to investigate ways they can target the network itself or how to setup fake base stations, but so far haven't succeeded in creating a wholesale breach to lots of users.

The traditional mobile network has always been an attractive target for attack but as described in the history part of this book, design changes over the years have made it an increasingly hard target to break.

There have been a number of published theoretical attacks by security researchers and cryptanalysts on how to break the security of mobile networks but the resilience of networks so far has been reasonably strong and is continuing to develop in that sense. Changes in network architecture and the deployment into non-protected environments such as people's homes may change this (4G takes mobile networks to an 'all IP' world meaning that everything talks in the language of the internet which is very well understood by the bad guys). When travelling abroad it is wise to remember that not all countries allow any encryption on the mobile network so the conversations you have and the messages you send may be visible to the authorities, but it really depends on your own particular security needs and how much you trust the country you're visiting.

5.11.3   Bluetooth

Bluetooth is contained in this section, although it is mostly not used for traditional 'networking'. It can be if a device is 'tethered' wirelessly to provide internet through a phone to a computer. Bluetooth is a short-range wireless feature which is standard on nearly all phones. There have been a number of published attacks on Bluetooth which targeted voice headset connections, extracted phonebooks from insecure devices and enabled malicious messages to be sent to unsuspecting users. Viruses and worms have also been transmitted over Bluetooth. All of these attacks generally date back to the early days of Bluetooth and the newer standards and implementations are generally secure against these kinds of problems. Manufacturers have removed some of the logical flaws which would help such attacks (such as not asking the user for permission when something happens). Nevertheless, Bluetooth still exists as a potential attack vector and researchers are always interested in any entry point to a phone. As a rule, if you don't need a feature like Bluetooth on, leave it off. You are then secure by default.

5.12   Network Guidelines

- However tempting it may be to connect to free WiFi when you're out and about, take a moment to consider who is providing that service and why. If they're charging, who are you giving your credit card details to?

- Don't connect to a hotspot that is completely unencrypted or which uses WEP encryption as this provides no confidentiality at all.

- By connecting to an untrusted network, you could potentially allow an attacker to get into your accounts for social networking sites, your email and banking details. In general if you are connected to a public WiFi network, don't do anything sensitive such as internet banking or making purchases.

- Consider using a VPN service for your internet connections over WiFi.

6   Malware

Malware refers to applications that can be installed on devices which are likely to cause some form of harm to the user. It covers a multitude of things from viruses, Trojans and Spyware - all of which are covered here, but also could refer to applications that unintentionally cause harm by just being badly written.

Mobile malware has been with us since 2004, albeit in a very small form. Mobile anti-virus has been around for about the same amount of time. The solution to a problem that largely didn't exist was being sold by an industry that had a vested interest in there actually being a problem. This was and still continues to be, a dangerous situation. Back in 2005, one anti-virus vendor was trying to sell a mobile solution. They had an application that completely filled the phone's application memory – a good solution perhaps as the user couldn't install anything else! The mobile industry was a new market for anti-virus vendors and virus writers – the PC market was saturated for anti-virus and those companies needed to make money. In addition, the security on PCs was getting to the point that it was difficult to create successful malware. What both these sets of people underestimated was the state of fragmentation in mobile platforms – that is, the differences between potential virus "hosts" in mobile phones were so great that it was difficult to create a piece of malware that would spread to a wide number of users. Not only this, but the security departments of the mobile phone companies were already one step ahead. The design of mobile phones took into account some of the mistakes that had happened in the past in the PC world and they had designed security measures to counter the main issues. A battle has been waged on two fronts – one is a messaging battle from the mobile industry that anti-virus is a waste of money[20] and the other which is tackling the bad guys who'd like to break all the security measures and find new ways in. Nowadays, we have much more open devices with incredible capabilities and a mobile market that has enough commonalities (such as the market being largely dominated by two platforms – Google's Android and Apple's iOS). This could, in theory add up to the perfect storm for a mass-malware outbreak, but it hasn't happened, mainly due to the measures the industry is taking to prevent it. Indeed, Apple has banned anti-virus applications from its app store, much to the frustration of some anti-virus companies[21], however Apple is not itself immune from malware issues but manages to still maintain the perception that it is[22].

Infection figures from anti-virus vendors have swayed around wildly and it is difficult to get a true picture from an industry that has a vested interest in there being a malware problem. The market situation around the world varies massively too. China and Russia report greater problems with mobile malware than the rest of the world. This is largely due to the characteristics of those markets (lots of unofficial app stores with no quality control, offering pirated applications and malware).

6.1 Types of Malware and Aims

There are many different types of malware with different aims. The word 'virus' is used quite a lot by the media and this seems to be a catch-all term, however a virus is specifically something that can self-replicate and this type of attack is almost impossible to execute on today's mobile devices due to the security design of the handsets.

Some of the terminology about different types of malware is explained below:

- Spyware – A type of malware that gathers data on a mobile phone without the user's knowledge. The types of data that mobile spyware can collect include not only call details and messages but even data from certain applications and audio recordings of the room you're in.

- Botnet – A number of devices that have lost control to a third party with malicious intentions, after having their security compromised. These devices can potentially then be controlled remotely to attack a particular target, en masse. A botnet is connected in some way to 'command & control'. On mobile this is sometimes done over SMS.

- Adware – An application that contains code to serve up advertisements to a user in a way that is deliberately confusing to the user, for example by giving alerts and notifications to the user, or by adding an icon. The data can also be gathered and used without the user's consent.

- Premium Rate – Calls or messages to numbers with significantly higher rates than the standard contract rates from the provider. These premium rate numbers are often used for competitions or charity donations (in the UK, this is regulated by PhonePayPlus[23]). Malicious applications can often make money for their masters this way – the author owns the premium rate number and collects the revenue.

- Rootkit – A software tool that gains full, unfettered access to the foundations of the mobile device, giving it privileged access to other things on the device and usually completely subverting any security feature or software installed on the device.

- Trojan Horse – Acts as a legitimate application, but instead performs harmful tasks without the user's consent as it has some badness hidden within. Users can often be lured into installing trojanised applications. For example, fake free games or infected pirated versions.

6.2 Some Interesting Malware

This section describes some interesting malware that has been found and shows certain features which may point to future trends. The threat from malware remains extremely low, despite there being many years of research by criminals and the hacking community. This is largely down to security measures taken inside devices and proactive mechanisms by app store owners to prevent and deal with malware once it manifests itself. Many types of malware are just modifications of existing ones that have worked (the code can get distributed through private hacking forums). Sometimes this is a deliberate technique to keep ahead of anti-virus vendors' software which largely still relies on 'signatures' of malware, so modifying an app very slightly can result in the malware going undetected. The number of real, unique strains of malware is still quite low, but the industry is wise not to be complacent as there is a real determination to attack mobile.

6.2.1 Name: Cabir

Operating System: Symbian S60 2nd Edition

Description: This was the first 'proper' virus on a mobile phone. It distributes itself via Bluetooth, so it is technically a "worm". It was released as a proof of concept virus by a Russian group called 29a.

6.2.2   Name: Skulls

Operating System: Symbian S60 2nd Edition

Description: Created by Tee-222, replaces applications on the C: with new ones. Malicious AIF (Application info and icon) file – the icons are all skull and crossbones and the application pointer points to nowhere so the user interface is disabled.

6.2.3   Name: Commwarrior

Operating System: Symbian

Description: A malicious application that originated in Russia. It makes copies of itself and tries to send them over Bluetooth to any nearby devices and sends copies to the entire phonebook of the device. This was probably the most effective malware on Symbian. There have been lots of different variants over the years – the displayed names of the application when it infects change to plausible things that a user may be enticed to install.

6.2.4   Name: Flexispy

Operating System: Symbian, Android, WinCE, iOS (jailbroken)

Description: This was the first commercially available spyware for phones and is still sold today. The original version would take a copy of all SMSs and call logs and send this information to a server which the attacker would have access to. The latest versions have much more features – including the ability to read emails, instant messaging, the phonebook, location and even record conversations and phone calls. The iPhone version only works on jailbroken devices and neither iPhone nor Android versions are available through the official app stores as they violate the app store policies. The authors of Flexispy have been quite aggressive towards anti-virus vendors who are blocking their application within devices, even though quite clearly the user of the phone is in all likelihood not going to know that Flexispy is on there. As a result, Flexispy is classified as 'riskware' in some versions of the application rather than 'spyware'. The reasons behind this are fairly complex. One definition of spyware is that it 'self-installs', whereas Flexispy must be installed by a physical person and has an installation page on the phone. However, any sensible person will realise that as the purpose of the application is to spy on other people, then that software could be installed by someone with access to the phone. If that person is a jealous partner, then they have

40

considerable access. There are many different types of spyware applications just like Flexispy for various devices.

6.2.5   Name: DroidDream

Operating System: Android

Description: A Trojan that is added to pirated Android applications. These applications were uploaded to the Android market (now called Google Play). The malicious Trojan code does some quite bad things. It uses a 'root exploit' called RageAgainstTheCage which gives it elevated privileges to sensitive permissions on the phone. It then harvests users' personal information. It also had the ability to update itself. Google were forced to remove these applications from the market and infected devices. Shortly after, they introduced further measures to prevent pollution of the market with such applications. This was probably one of the most advanced pieces of malware found in the official app store and it had been downloaded by thousands of users. Google reacted extremely quickly to deal with it, but it was still after the event.

6.2.6   Name: ZitMo (Zeus in the Mobile)

Operating System: Symbian, Android, Blackberry

Description: This malware is particularly important as it was the first time that a mainstream, widely used computer botnet had targeted mobile devices. The versions on mobile have been quite clumsy and rely on a heavy social engineering of the user to get them to install the application due to the security restrictions in place on mobile devices.

The attack is combined with the computer-based Zeus banking botnet which there are many variants of around the world, on a huge number of infected PCs[24]. One of the weaknesses of Zeus and its variants is that it has to wait until the point at which the user logs onto their online banking before it can do nasty things (intercepting transactions). The introduction of messages sent to users' mobiles by the banks offered a new attack vector which would make things easier. The attack required both the user's PC and their mobile to be infected.

ZitMo intercepts mTANs (Mobile Transaction Authentication Numbers) that are sent over SMS which are basically one-time passwords sent to your mobile while you are performing online banking on your computer, to confirm it is actually you doing the online banking (two-factor authentication). This is part of some bank systems in countries such as Germany and Spain. The SMSs are then sent back by ZitMo to the command and control server. The attacker then uses that information to perform transactions on a computer somewhere else, without the user ever needing to log-on to their banking account.

The application is also controlled by a command and control server so that it can be remotely commanded to do things over SMS such as change who is controlling it and so on[25].

The overall attack is so sophisticated that when a user checks their online banking accounts on their PC, the displayed fraudulent transactions are removed by the malware, so the user cannot see that something has happened. The first they'll know is when they go to a bank machine and see that their balance is different.

The sophistication of the attack and others such as those using another botnet, SpyEye[26] shows a determination to attack online banking via mobile as well as these new types of hybrid computer/mobile attacks. It is expected that research by hacking groups will increase as banks' confidence to deploy mobile applications grows.

6.2.7 Name: RuFraud

Operating System: Android

Description: This malware was hidden in 27 seemingly legitimate and popular Android applications such as "downloaders" for Angry Birds in Google's app store. The way it works is by sending SMS messages to a premium rate number when the app is opened (three messages at £5 each). It then deletes messages that are associated with the fraud (sent and received), for example those that would inform the user that they have been charged. This means that the victim doesn't realise until they get their bill[26].

The premium rate regulator in the UK, PhonePayPlus fined the Latvian creators behind it £50,000 and forced them to refund the customers the money they had been charged. Disappointingly, no arrests were made as the authors were not in the UK, which may have been part of the fraudsters' tactics. As a measure of how low infection rates are in countries like the UK, only 34 customers complained. Obviously this is only a proportion of the users who would have been affected, but it is still tiny in comparison with the population of smartphones in the country[27].

6.2.8   Name: DroidKungFu

Operating System: Android

Description: Another example of malware which uses 'rootkit' exploits is DroidKungFu. It was capable of rooting Android phones and avoiding detection from any anti-virus software present. It has been found on a handful of trojanised applications, circulated on Chinese forums. The malware contains two encrypted root exploits (udev and RageAgainstTheCage) to mask their inclusion from any detection software on installation. Once running, the malware decrypts the exploits and then proceeds to execute them. This ultimately opens up a backdoor in the device so that it can be controlled as part of a botnet and can remotely remove data, delete files and run other applications.

Although this attack happened in China which has a high number of poorly policed application stores and a high number of counterfeit devices, it shows the level of sophistication in terms of malware development. Again, a root exploit was used to gain higher levels of privilege which allows the attacker to 'own' the device beneath the application layer where anti-virus would be running, meaning it can run completely undetected with full access to everything.

6.3   What is Jailbreaking and Rooting?

The devices that manufacturers sell today are generally attached to an application ecosystem which is very well controlled compared with the PC world. This new world has many benefits for users in that they can generally source applications from a clean environment which has at least (some) checking taking place that the applications that are being offered are not harmful.

This also helps to prevent a lot of piracy. Although piracy still exists (even within the app stores themselves), it is less than in the PC world. It also stifles some innovation as certain types of application are not allowed, or the capabilities required to do certain things are restricted for security reasons. One anti-virus vendor even encourages their users to root their devices in order to enable a firewall feature! Certain communities have grown to provide additional functionality, enhanced applications and even complete bespoke operating systems have been created which run with a different look and feel[28]. Not all of this innovation is desirable for users and the majority of effort is applied to cracking and pirating applications from within app stores and providing them free. Complete competing app store 'type' ecosystems exist such as Cydia for Apple[29].

As such, there is a strong incentive for even legitimate users to root or jailbreak their devices, often driven by the desire to not pay for applications from Apple's App Store. Jailbreaking is the terminology used for breaking out of the security sandbox on iOS devices. Rooting is usually used in terms of Android devices. For hackers 'getting root' on a Linux-based device means they can usually completely own the device and can do anything they want. It is very difficult to detect. The term 'rootkit' is used in reference to malware that does this – getting to the lowest level of the computing system, below application-level security checking provided by anti-virus tools or by the system itself. Demonstration 'rootkits' for mobile have been created that target application frameworks to allow installation and replacement of existing applications (such as a fake web browser)[30].

So there are benefits and drawbacks to jailbreaking or rooting your device. On the one-hand the user will be able to install cracked applications and new features they wouldn't have been able to get 'inside' the normal ecosystem provided to consumers, on the other hand the user who does this is removing any hope of protecting themselves from some very serious threats – they've removed the security foundations of the operating system and are engaging in very risky behaviour. It is strongly recommended that users do not root or jailbreak devices. Not only this, but it will void the warranty on the device. An easy example of how bad this can be is the functionality that is granted to programmes like Flexispy in the rooted / jailbroken versions. They are able to do much more – if you as a user had already rooted your device, it makes it much easier for an attacker to take advantage of you with spyware. These attacks could also be more easily executed through the browser as you've already done half the work for the attacker.

6.4 What Devices are affected by Mobile Malware?

All devices can theoretically be affected by malware. Malware is primarily prevalent on so-called smart-phones (those which applications can be installed on), but it is even theoretically possible but extremely difficult (and therefore not worthwhile) to create malicious software for closed operating systems for phones. As of writing, the only smartphone operating system on the market today that has not been successfully targeted with malware appears to be Windows Phone (the new operating system used on newer Nokia devices such as the Lumia 900). A proof of concept piece of malware has been demonstrated by an Indian hacker but that is all so far. This is due to the relatively low maturity of the operating system and low market uptake although it contains some good security features.

6.5 How Mobile Malware Infections Occur

6.5.1 Peer-to-peer packages

As a UK consumer, probably the most likely way you are going to get infected is by using peer-to-peer services such as bit torrent to download large packages of games for free. These applications are often pirated and can also contain malware. The infection works because the user is incentivised to install the 'free' application, even though they know that they're generally committing piracy. The risk / reward is such that they're willing to do it and they may not actually be aware once the malware is on their device. To side-load to Android devices is relatively straightforward. The Android ecosystem is designed to be more open – it is up to the user if they want to side-load untrusted, non-Google Play applications.

6.5.2 Jailbroken devices and unofficial app stores

For Apple devices, the user must jailbreak their device and then use third party app stores such as Cydia (which derives from a reference to "a worm in the apple") to install unsigned applications which haven't been checked by Apple. As mentioned above, the problem is that once the device is jailbroken, high levels of privileges are granted to any application on the device, meaning that as a user you are at a much higher level of risk than you were with the legitimate build of software. It has also shown up some interesting problems with Apple – the open source community are able to move much more quickly than big companies. In 2010, a pdf security vulnerability was identified through a jailbreaking trick. Ironically Cydia users were able to patch their devices to close the hole, however normal Apple users were vulnerable for some time. Cydia itself just acts a link through to repositories of applications so users just have to rely on the reputation of repositiories. Users often don't review application dependencies (which would reveal any potentially malicious behaviour by an app) as it is not straightforward to do. Users of Cydia who installed certain packages (OpenSSH for example) left themselves open to attack by not changing the Apple default root password of "alpine". A worm[31] and botnet[32] were subsequently created which worked against these jailbroken devices. Cydia and its like tend to have to police themselves. An issue in the summer of 2012 where a developer included adware into some applications was reported by a member of the Cydia community and dealt with by the repository owner, developer and the owner of Cydia. No reason was given for the original behaviour or what specific things were said to the developer to make him change his behavior[33]. Known spyware is available for jailbroken iPhone devices such as Flexispy (described in this book).

There are even rumours that some devices being bought on ebay have been deliberately pre-loaded with malware. Something similar to this has happened in the PC world where pirated copies of operating systems were unwittingly pre-installed on laptops in the factory, that were then sold through legitimate sources to customers.

6.5.3   Infection via app store

As discussed elsewhere in this book, the likelihood of infection from an official application store is low, however it is not impossible. As shown in the examples of malware above, some of these have been discovered by concerned consumers in app stores. App stores that are more open such as Android Play carry a greater risk as they want as much innovation to happen. The Apple app store is much more tightly controlled, but errors do still happen. The important thing is more about detecting an issue as early as possible and reacting to it quickly such that the impact on consumers is minimised. The development of various features on the app store side for dealing with this has helped to create a very safe overall environment for consumers in places like the UK. In some countries however, there aren't any 'official' app stores from the main players and consumers are exposed to all sorts of malware applications that simply don't work.

6.5.4   Physical access

There are some people who will say that security only extends as far as the attacker not having physical access to the device. This is true to a certain extent. For example, if the person wanting to install Spyware on your device is your partner or spouse, there is considerable opportunity for that person to get access to your device when it is unattended. It does depend on the capability of the attacker. Most people can install an application so taking basic precautions against other people getting access to do that is a basic and important precaution. On Apple devices users can't side-load an application onto the device anyway so an attacker has to take more extreme steps. On Android devices however, it is possible to do this by enabling the security option for installing applications from "unknown sources" (that is not originating from Google Play, where Spyware is forbidden)[34]. A malicious person could therefore install a piece of Spyware on a Google device if they have the ability to get into the menus of the device. In security parlance, this is called a "lunch-time attack". The idea being that, leaving your phone or computer unattended for a period of time allows the attacker to get in. The onus is on the user to prevent any form of extended access to the device. Many access features are available on the device (some discussed later). There are more advanced forms of Spyware, for which the attacker needs to root the device or jailbreak it (for Apple). In all cases, reducing the amount of time your phone is unattended and 'open' rather than having security protections enabled is absolutely critical.

In one proof-of-concept test at a hacking conference, hackers built a free battery charging station and placed it in the corridor of the conference centre. Lured in by the need to charge their phones, people plugged in the micro-USB chargers to their devices. Little known to them was the fact that the USB chargers were in fact connected to a PC which then managed to extract all the data from the devices.

6.6   Is Malware a Big Risk?

The current situation for malware could be described as 'overblown'. In the UK, the risk of infection for a normal user, who doesn't engage in risky behaviour such as installing apps that aren't from official distribution channels is very low. In other countries this is not the case. Lookout claims in their "State of Mobile Security 2012" report[35] that "Android malware likelihood is much higher in Russia, Ukraine and China than elsewhere. In terms of user behaviour, people who download apps outside of trusted sources like Google Play have a higher likelihood of encountering malware." This is an extremely important point that anti-virus vendors will not often tell their consumers. If you are normal user, downloading applications from the official App Stores such as Google Play, the risk you are running is extremely low.

Some mobile security companies who work with mobile operators are reporting declines in the amount of mobile malware. This is significant because those companies have access to real traffic rather than basing their stats on a limited subset of users.

The flawed malware statistics and blatant scare sales tactics have created a distorted situation which also runs the risk of a 'cry wolf' effect amongst consumers. However, as can be seen in the malware examples in this book, malicious applications have been becoming more sophisticated and it is by no means a certainty that the industry will hold out against a massive 'class' attack that will break millions of devices. It is clear that in countries such as China that there is a big mobile malware problem which can be attributable to lots of uncontrolled application markets which are more akin to low-quality street markets in terms of the applications available within them. Also hampering the situation in China is the number of unofficial 'forks' of the Android operating system which are sold in some official products but also in a lot of 'Shanzhai' or counterfeit products.

6.7 Developer Decisions

A bigger problem than malware is poorly written applications. Although App Stores can perform some level of checking to check that something isn't blatantly malicious, it would take a lot of human intervention to physically inspect every application.

Most developers aren't incentivised to think a great deal about the internal security of their applications or what they're exposing their users to. Implementing security is hard and many developers and companies think they can get away without it unless something goes wrong, then they'll fix it. This can also be applied to attitudes around user data privacy.

The biggest incentive to fix security or not escalate the number of requested permissions is 'blowback' from users who give poor ratings for an application if it asks for strange permissions – for example requesting location or access to phonebook permissions in a simple game. However on some platforms (the iPhone being the main one), you don't necessarily know what permissions are being requested, so as a user you're none the wiser and have to assume that Apple are properly inspecting applications.

A few examples have highlighted this issue. In early 2012, an application called 'Path' for the iPhone uploaded users' phonebooks to their servers for "friend finding and matching". This was investigated by a user who uncovered the fact that all the information was being sent over without the end-user's permission. It was also being sent in its raw form rather than using a better method of scrambling it to not reveal the exact information when it was stored[36]. In addition, it had managed to get into the Apple App Store, despite violating rules stating that the user's permission should be requested before uploading such information. Path was eventually forced to upload a new version of the application which requested the user's permission before uploading their address book.

Address book uploading is emerging as quite a common feature in applications in order to increase the viral spread of an application (and therefore its success)[37]. In the case of Path, they uploaded each contact card rather than just the phone number, so the data included email addresses, job titles and any other information that may be included in contact cards such as birthdays and so on. This is the data of other people, not the users themselves!

This may come at a big price for users in the future, who are once again giving away all of the data that they own at the click of a button. Not only is this mainly just serving the interests of the company providing the application rather than the user, but the developers can pay fast and loose with the data. If a company is too lazy to implement encryption between your device and their servers, do you trust that they will keep your data secure from other things such as a cyber-attack against their company which exposes all the information?

Vodafone has taken a strong lead along with the GSMA in developing privacy guidelines for developers[38]. These documents cover not just the primary functions of an application that requires customer data usage, but also secondary uses of data such as for marketing purposes and education about data that is either intentionally or unintentionally being gathered[39].

6.8   How App Stores Protect Users

Official application stores protect their users through a variety of mechanisms. Apple does not allow anti-virus software into their App Store, which has upset those companies which sell such software. It also allows the myth to perpetuate that the iPhone (and Apple) is invulnerable to security issues. There are good reasons not to allow such applications in the App Store though. Many of the permissions needed by security software solutions are the very same that are needed to cripple the device by malware authors. After all, how else would an anti-virus vendor be able to scan a device and inspect all the applications? If those permissions were granted to third parties, it would certainly prise open the door to malware developers. Whilst Apple's solutions are a lot more locked down than their competitors, they have still suffered issues but do a good job on the PR side of addressing security perceptions amongst the general public. The public has no other option but to expect that Apple continue to protect them responsibly. This section explains some of the mechanisms that the various app stores use to protect their customers.

6.8.1   Developer validation

The first thing that they do is validate that the developer of an application actually exists. This can be quite difficult, but can require a combination of supplying credit card details, verification of an account (for example iTunes which links back to home address etc.). Other systems require the user to get a digital certificate issued by a selected provider. This involves an identification validation service to check that the person is who they say they are. Once a certificate is issued, this can be used for signing each application a developer creates. The overall system for developer validation has holes that can be exploited, but has seen relatively low abuse (at least that has been publicly acknowledged).

6.8.2   Digital signing

Most application ecosystems require a developer to digitally sign their application. This provides a couple of things. It says that the contents of the application are what they were at the time of signing (i.e. that someone hasn't intercepted the application somewhere and modified its contents). This is usually also used for any updates to the application in the future. It also gives the app store a form of proof of integrity - if the application was bad, then that was indeed what was submitted. It also gives a limited form of authenticity – that the application was signed by this person. Of course this can't necessarily be proved, but the keys needed to sign each application have to be held securely by the developer and not shared with other people.

6.8.3   Static and dynamic analysis

Most application stores perform both static and dynamic analysis of submitted applications. That is to look at the code before it is run (statically) for anything that could be bad and to also run the application in a safe environment to see what happens (dynamically). It is necessary to perform this testing automatically to deal with the sheer volume of submitted applications. There are different indicators that can quickly show whether something is malicious. For example, any application that sends SMS could potentially be trying to send to a premium rate number. If this is combined with calls to other 'sensitive' features such as the phonebook or access to private data, the risk factor increases and it may be that the application is escalated for human testing to check that it really isn't malicious. Other application behaviours are also analysed. Google's main system for analysing applications (along with other techniques they use) is called 'Bouncer'. Obviously this means that attackers will try and target Bouncer and its ilk to try and subvert it. Security researchers have proven that they can successfully work their way around Bouncer and this work has been published, forcing Google to tighten up procedures[40]. The objective for a successful attack is to hide their activity in such a way that it looks like legitimate activity. For example, an application that the user expects to be sending SMSs such as a voting application could violate this trust by sending private information or send premium rate messages.

6.8.4   Peer-review

Application ecosystems like Android rely on their millions of users to review applications amongst themselves. They also provide links to report something that is potentially malicious. Although reviews by users can provide an excellent base of testers and immediate feedback on things that are malicious, there have been questions about the responsiveness to reports of malware. Sometimes applications have been reported as malware and it has taken months for them to be removed from an application store.

6.8.5   Application removal and the kill switch

If something is identified as malicious, the official application stores can very quickly remove the offending application from sale and download. They also have in extreme circumstances the ability to remotely remove an application from a handset. This is very rarely used and in order to respect users, they will be asked for confirmation. An example of the kill switch in action can be seen where security researcher Jon Oberheide's applications were being 'killed' by Google[41].

Remote removal is popularly known as the "kill switch". Google call their tool the Remote Application Removal Feature"[42]. In March 2011, Google reportedly removed 58 malicious applications from the then-called Google Market and used the kill switch to remotely remove them from 260,000 affected devices. They also remotely added a tool which would clean-up the devices[43].

6.9   Permissions in Applications

Permissions have been discussed a lot in this section and mobile platforms have a long way to go to get to a better way of handling access to sensitive features. Users don't have the ability to revoke permission to an application that they've previously given access to, say their location unless they turn the GPS function off entirely (which is a sensible thing to do as a general rule when you don't need it). While the permissions problem is still not solved in mobile, it is important that users pay attention to what they're giving access to. In the Apple world, users don't get the ability beyond giving access to the phonebook or location, but in Android devices, users should always think about what an application is supposed to be doing, where it came from and who made it. Simple internet searches can often verify the validity of an application if you suspect all is not well. Inspect the permissions that an application requests. Does this application really need access to your phonebook? Does it really need to send SMSs? If not, just don't install it. Phone permissions can be difficult to understand, so even a legitimate application can give a misleading impression of what it actually does. There are some tools available to help you manage your permissions, for example only giving one application the permission to get to your location.

6.10 Third-party Security and Protection Software

Anti-virus is a poor term for the tools that are provided by third party security companies who have traditionally provided exactly that on PCs. The problem has been that the industry themselves have made a lot of noise about viruses on mobile in order to scare people into downloading protection they generally don't need. The effectiveness of such anti-virus is also questionable given the methods used by attackers (a lot of which have been mentioned in this book). A more sensible approach would have been to concentrate on the whole host of other really good features that they provide in such 'mobile security protection suites'.

Features often provided include:

- Child protection –
    - o for websites and applications (such as by applying age restrictions or whitelists of 'safe websites')
    - o Allowing parents to lock down installation of new applications and only allowing certain applications to be run
- Helping users with lost or stolen devices –
    - o Locking the device, remote wiping and locating
    - o Activation of an alarm
    - o Locking the phone when the SIM is changed and sending a message to the user
- Blocking of phone numbers and messages (incoming and outgoing)
    - o Blocking premium rate numbers
- Preventing malware and "harmful" applications (the anti-virus part!)
- Safe browsing – avoid going to websites that are known to be malicious and harmful
- Identity protection features

As can be seen, these supplementary features can be really helpful (although some are usually built into phones anyway such as lost device tracking and disabling). Manufacturers don't tend to get involved in areas such as child protection or safe web-browsing, so these third party companies can really add value to users in terms of overall safe and secure usage.

Some of the more responsible security companies include Lookout[6], Symantec[44] and F-Secure[45] all of whom provide mobile security applications.

6.11   Device Manufacturer and Operating System Security

The device manufacturers and operating system vendors have a lot of experience in dealing with hackers targeting their devices and software. Over the years the mobile industry has continually worked to improve the underlying hardware security of devices to prevent really nefarious embedded systems hacking. Mobile devices are therefore much more secure than their PC equivalents. What started out as measures to protect against hackers targeting the SIMlock of phones and changing the identity of a phone (the IMEI number) after theft has created a solid foundation for protecting other things. This includes banking transactions and the application framework on devices. Of course the hacking groups themselves have not remained static which is why there are rooting tools and various hacks still coming available. As the technology has grown to include many other features such as premium video content, payments and a whole host of other things, so it has attracted the attention of attackers who would have traditionally never have come near mobile. As everything converges on the mobile device, so does the threat. Security issues can always be found, but it is the scale and impact of those security issues that really matters. The inherent protection given to users within the device itself is largely unseen by them but it has ensured that the mobile industry has still not suffered a really critical security incident, despite repeated attempts by criminals and hackers. This book does not discuss these measures in detail, but it is important to be aware that if the foundations of a device are not secured, nothing above it can be secure. Leading edge security technologies are already being implemented in devices that provide the next generation of what is called 'trusted computing' type technologies, which are really strong Trusted Execution Environments combined with Secure Storage on phones.

6.12 Malware and Application Guidelines

- Don't install untrusted applications or those from unknown sources such as those downloaded from an internet forum. The majority of malware that exists in the mobile world is spread this way.

- Don't install applications provided through links that come through Twitter or Facebook – they invariably don't link back to the official version in the market.

  o This is also a technique that is used to try and dupe users to install malware.

- Don't root or jailbreak your phone - you are removing security measures designed to protect you and you cannot be certain what is running on your device or what it is doing.

- Always review the permissions fully before you install an application. If you're not completely happy, don't install it and have a look on the web to find out more about what the application does and what people are saying about it.

- Be very careful of applications that want access to your entire phonebook:

  o Applications such as WhatsApp are incredibly popular but the way that they discover connections is by mapping all your phonebook entries to other users' data they have collected – all sat on their servers, in another country. If these applications collect all this data, what other phone numbers do you have in your phonebook? The office number? Sensitive contacts? Is this data being sent in-the-clear across the internet instead of being encrypted?

  o If in doubt, do some internet research on the application you're thinking of using and see if they actively secure your data. What are the bad things that people are saying about the application?

- Make sure you don't have options selected you don't need:

  o Turn off NFC, Bluetooth and location if you're not using them

  o Don't allow installation of 'unknown sources'

  o Don't turn on developer options

7 Strength-in-Depth and Defence Techniques

Mobile phone security isn't all about the bad parts, there are good elements too! There is wealth of experience across the mobile phone industry in dealing with security issues. As discussed in the previous section, this has been building up over the years as attacks become more sophisticated and new functionality that has security requirements converges onto devices that have security requirements. Ten years ago, the average security professional working in the mobile industry didn't have to deal with banking security issues or have to be thinking about cars! In addition, with the opening up of mobile devices to third party developers, some great innovative applications have emerged which really help consumers to be more secure. The way to think about security on your device is to build up strength in depth. For example if a thief steals your device and it is PIN-locked, that is one thing, but what if it isn't? You need to think about what the next step is. Protecting the data on the device using encryption or a protection application and having enabled the remote disabling feature makes you feel a lot more comfortable in advance of a theft and certainly after it. Equally, using the security features provided with your device will help you a lot. These days they are highly configurable – you can usually set the time-out on a screen lock so that it is set to something that is usable for you and not too annoying, but will be useful when it matters. It only takes a little while to sit down and set these things up, but it could help prevent a security incident and help you to react effectively if there is one.

Remember also that there are things that you can do to help yourself, just by engaging in safe behaviours. For example, it probably isn't advisable to give your child your phone to play with – children don't have the ability to make the decisions that you will and they certainly won't realise the implications if they cause a security problem on your works' phone. If you're using a work issued handset, follow the rules that you've been set by your organisation or company, such as not reading sensitive documents on trains or taking it with you on holiday if you don't need to. In general, try to minimise your risk exposure – turning off unused or rarely used features on the device will also save you battery life. If you can develop a security habit, you'll be a lot safer, but try to be pragmatic about it!

7.1   Defensive Measures Guidelines

- Device Encryption - Depending on your security needs, some devices such as newer Android phones have built-in full device encryption. This can be cumbersome to use as you will need to enter the password you have chosen each time you unlock your device, but it gives a much higher level of security. If your phone is stolen it is near impossible for anyone to get access to the data.

- Setting the delay for the screen-lock to activate is a feature of some handsets and can be tailored to your own particular needs. This is really useful as each person is different. When setting the delay, try to get a balance between what you feel is useful and your own security needs. If someone grabs your handset from a café table, will the security lock be enabled?

- Try to resist the temptation to give your child your work phone. They might install more than you bargained for.

- Follow the rules laid out by your organisation's device usage policy – you don't know who you're sat next to on the train.

8　Future technologies

We are still just at the start of the mobile revolution. There is much more functionality to be integrated into devices and probably many different new physical form factors to come. On the near horizon, we have some pretty big changes coming. This section discusses some of these and what impact they'll have.

8.1　Mobile Payments and Banking

There are many different flavours of mobile payments already existing on mobile. For example, you can purchase a TV using Amazon one-click through your mobile's browser. In a lot of developing countries, mobile payments are massive, particularly amongst those who don't have bank accounts. The Vodafone backed M-Pesa is dominant amongst lots of others. When people generally think about m-payments in the UK, they're looking forward to the day when NFC-enabled payments exist on mobile. Google Wallet offers this in the USA, however the more popular system is something called Square which uses the phone's headphone jack to convert the data from a magnetic stripe reader into something the phone can understand. In Europe we have chip-and-pin so it is not possible to use Square. iZettle is another similar system which does work with chip-and-pin[46]. It has recently launched in the UK and is likely to become popular. The commercial wrangling over who controls the customer between the banks and network operators has delayed the technological rollout of true NFC-enabled payments although most new devices now have in-built NFC and even a lot of point-of-sale terminals in shops have the capability because of NFC chips in bank cards. It remains to be seen how consumers will take to it. One aspect of 'touch' payments that is different is that transactions below £15 will not require PIN entry. This is enough to be attractive to thieves so there could potentially be a rise in street crime. There could also be increases in violent crime where users are forced to empty their mobile wallets for thieves.

8.2   Biometrics

Biometrics is the mechanism by which a system uses something about you to identify and authenticate you, allowing you access. On mobile, there have been some attempts at using biometrics, but they have mostly failed for various reasons, not least because of the practicality of using them. A few years ago, there was a mobile phone with a fingerprint scanner and the latest versions of Android (Ice Cream Sandwich) have a "face unlock" feature. Things like face unlock are so unfriendly to use that they are no more than a gimmick. In fact, some previous versions could be defeated by a photograph of the phone's owner. There have also been some quite effective attacks against fingerprint scanners too. The processing power needed to perform really strong, reliable biometric authentication is very high and as yet isn't really practical for an offline mechanism for getting into your phone.

Human beings are difficult to work with and biometrics can be described as a "socially regressive" technology. For example, fingerprint scanning doesn't work for a large number of people – the young, the very old, manual workers, some disabled people and the list goes on. It is difficult to use things like voice recognition in a public environment.

The last issue with biometrics is a society one. There have been some quite brutal attacks on people in the past who have had biometric systems[47] and people tortured and then murdered for their PINs[48]. By putting the security onto the user that much, are we going to cause more harm to people than good?

8.3   Web Applications, Device and Network APIs

The increasing connectivity of devices has meant that the web part of mobile devices has become the most important component. So much so that companies are developing entire devices that are based on the web. There have been various attempts to develop this in the past few years, but the most recently active project is Mozilla and Telefonica's Open Web Device. This will be initially launched in Latin America and will be built on top of an Android base, but every application will effectively be a self-contained website. Developments in web technology and the new standard for the future web: HTML5, mean that web applications will look and feel a lot more like the traditional 'native' applications of today's smartphones. The connected nature of these web applications will mean more dynamic data from the web can be put together to enhance the user experience. To further enhance this, sets of 'device APIs' which open up key underlying features of phones such as location functions or the phonebook are being implemented. The worrying thing is that the rush towards providing great usability and functionality is sacrificing user privacy and security. The permissions model doesn't work for native applications, so it is even worse in the web world which is much less secure. Not only this, but 'network APIs' are being provided too which will give companies access to the back-end systems of network operators to provide things like in-app billing and more detailed information on customer and location. The future in this area could be quite bleak for the mobile industry and users, unless companies begin to recognise what they are doing is extremely risky and take appropriate countermeasures. Web-related security problems caused by issues in browser runtime engines have happened in the past and will certainly happen again.

8.4   Bring Your Own Device (BYOD)

BYOD is a new term for policies that are being put in place in a lot of organisations that allow users to bring in their own phones and tablets to work. Although touted as being beneficial to users, it saves costs for the company and ultimately means that employees will work harder and longer. Often companies will have a written policy around how the device should be used and what you should and shouldn't do in regard to work time and work material on the device. This will be accompanied by some form of management application on the phone which you will have installed by your IT department (who will have a management tool on the company server side). This might govern the types of things you can access at certain times (just as on corporate issued BlackBerrys that may prevent application installation or access to features like the camera). It also allows the corporation to deal with lost handsets. Lots of issues start to emerge such as whether the company should be allowed to wipe your own device or not and what applications you can and cannot have on your phone. The concept is still developing but it looks like it is here to stay.

8.5   Machine-to-Machine (M2M)

Machine-to-machine communications already exist today but most people have just slipped into using such systems without realising it. In most home improvement stores you can buy systems that allow you to get SMS updates on home security or control light switches remotely. There are even SMS controlled door locks available. The growth of this type of technology is going to accelerate considerably, with predictions of 10s of billions of devices by 2020. 'Smart Meters' are able to talk back to the utility companies and perform remote readings. Lamp posts can be remotely and wirelessly turned on or off. Ordinary white goods are being developed that can tell the owner their status or even be turned on remotely. These M2M devices are forming the cornerstones of the 'Internet of Things' which is where everything is connected to the Internet and can interrelate. The security implications of this massively interconnected world are usually brushed over, but if one considers that a simple cyber-attack could theoretically empty every washing machine in the country, the scale of even a basic attack could destroy, for example, the insurance industry in one blow. Users will have to be even more careful with their mobile devices as they could literally be the keys to their house.

8.6   Automotive

Car manufacturers are already working on implementing mobile operating systems into cars. The idea is to enhance in-car entertainment and navigation initially, but this could lead as far as car control in the future. Being able to connect to the same operating system as your phone means that it will be easier to transfer data between the two systems and run the same applications using that data. The security implications are obvious and exist even now with Bluetooth connections that synchronise your phonebook to the car and store it there. Criminals have been known to take advantage of information stored in cars already with the 'Take Me Home' features of satellite navigation systems leading thieves to the car owner's home. It is clear that there will be many more issues in this area in the future.

8.7   Cloud Computing

'The cloud' is a marketing term for a lot of online services. Cloud services can include remote backup services and file storage (examples being things like DropBox or Google Drive), but it can refer to other online services. Facebook is essentially a cloud service as everything is stored on someone else's servers; nothing is really kept locally on your own devices. There can be some massive advantages to cloud computing. The plethora of mobile devices that people own means that having convenient access from each device to files, settings and historical information is incredibly useful for people. There are a lot of downsides too – companies relying on cloud services have found that when the cloud service goes down, their company literally grinds to a halt. If you're relying on that cloud service to get things right, you have to put a lot of trust in them. Recent years have seen cyber breaches that have resulted in hundreds of thousands of people's private data released into the wild and many celebrities have had their webmail accounts hacked and very private pictures released into the public domain. Cloud services will no doubt develop and security will get a lot better, but users should probably still be wary about constantly sending all their information over the internet when it probably doesn't need to be. The other aspect to consider (as has been previously mentioned in this document) is that it is not just your data. By giving away other people's contact details to a cloud service, you're potentially breaching their privacy as they may not wish for that data to be shared. Some companies have gone as far as to ban backup services like DropBox from being used by employees.

9 Summary and Author's Note

This book has provided an overview to a lot of the security issues facing users when it comes to using a mobile handset, its applications and various features. There are a number of guidelines listed which should help people when using phones to act in a safe and secure manner. At the end of the day, we're only human and mistakes do happen. If someone wants to target you for whatever reason, be it a jealous spouse or for cyber espionage reasons, if they are sufficiently determined they probably will succeed. However, for the vast majority of us it is the non-targeted attacks that can affect us. The accidental leakage of some credit card information over an open WiFi connection or the lost phone in a cab is much more likely and something we should be prepared for. These guidelines will hopefully be personally useful to you the reader, but it is important not to get scared of using new mobile technology. We're still only really at the beginning of the mobile world and it's something that is going to continue to enrich society and our own individual lives. Let's not let a few bad people take that away.

10 References

[1] Safe Kids worldwide survey:

http://www.safekids.org/assets/docs/safety-basics/safety-tips-by-risk-area/Walking-Safely-Research-Report.pdf

[2] RAC Foundation research:

http://www.racfoundation.org/assets/rac_foundation/content/downloadables/texting%20whilst%20driving%20-%20trl%20-%20180908%20-%20report.pdf:

[3] PanicGuard personal safety application:

http://panicguard.com/

[4] The Suzy Lamplugh Trust list of "Lone Worker Devices":

http://www.suzylamplugh.org/personal-safety-tips/lone-worker-directory/

[5] "Find My iPhone":

http://itunes.apple.com/gb/app/find-my-iphone/id376101648?mt=8

[6] Lookout Mobile Security:

https://www.lookout.com/

[7] 'Dial M for mugging' article:

http://www.standard.co.uk/lifestyle/london-life/dial-m-for-mugging--how-to-stop-iphone-robbers-and-keep-your-data-safe-too-8289062.html

[8] Tetrus Telecoms fine:

http://www.independent.co.uk/money/insurance/ppi-texts-firm-is-banned-by-advertising-watchdog-8418298.html

[9] Estimates of counterfeit Ugandan phones:

http://www.gbooza.com/forum/topics/30-of-ugandans-use-fake-phones#axzz2HIW0bRWN

[10] Counterfeit devices: "Blockberry":

http://www.engadget.com/2009/06/18/keepin-it-real-fake-part-ccxvii-not-even-obama-can-sell-us-on/

[11] Verrus paybyphone parking service:

http://shkspr.mobi/blog/index.php/2011/09/paying-for-parking-via-qr-code/

[12] QRjacking:

http://notdanwilkerson.wordpress.com/2011/05/03/qr-jacking/

[13] Security Assessment of Mobile QR Readers:

https://appsec-labs.com/blog/security-assessment-of-mobile-qr-readers-%E2%80%93-a-comparison

[14] Using QR Tags to Attack Smartphones:

http://kaoticoneutral.blogspot.co.uk/2011/09/using-qr-tags-to-attack-smartphones_10.html

[15] Pre-registration fraud:

http://shkspr.mobi/blog/index.php/2011/04/dear-nokia/

[16] Attacking NFC phones:

http://www.mulliner.org/nfc/feed/collin_mulliner_eusecwest08_attacking_nfc_phones.pdf

[17] Lastpass:

https://lastpass.com/

[18] Firesheep:

http://codebutler.com/firesheep/

[19] Norton Hotspot Privacy:

https://hotspot.norton.com/desktop/home.html

[20] What's next for mobile security:

http://www.guardian.co.uk/media-network/media-network-blog/2012/feb/29/mobile-security-droiddream-fear-uncertainty

[21] Kaspersky reaction to Apple's anti-virus app ban from App Store:

http://www.theregister.co.uk/2012/05/22/kaspersky_ios_antivirus/

[22] Is iPhone really malware free?:

http://anti-virus-rants.blogspot.co.uk/2012/02/is-iphone-really-malware-free.html

[23] PhonePayPlus:

http://www.phonepayplus.org.uk/

[24] Microsoft moves to disable Zeus botnet:

http://www.bbc.co.uk/news/technology-17515647

[25] Fortiguard:

http://blog.fortinet.com/eurograbber-is-zitmo/

[26] SpyEye:

http://www.trusteer.com/blog/first-spyeye-attack-android-mobile-platform-now-wild

[27] Fake Angry Bird app makers fined:

http://www.theregister.co.uk/2012/05/24/angry_birds_sms_scam_firm_fined/

[28] Cyanogenmod:

http://www.cyanogenmod.org/

[29] Cydia:

http://cydia.saurik.com/

[30] Smartphone image:

http://web.ncsu.edu/abstract/technology/wms-jiang-clickjack/

[31] Worm rickrolls unsecured jailbroken iPhones via SSH:

http://www.tuaw.com/2009/11/07/jailbreak-worm-rickrolls-the-unsecured/

[32] iPhone botnet:

http://www.machackpc.com/iphone-malware-%E2%80%93-iphoneibotnet-a/

[33] New adware / malware found in Cydia:

http://modmyi.com/forums/cydia-support/810633-new-adware-malware-found-cydia.html

[34] Google have introduced a basic virus scanning engine into the install from 'unknown sources' feature as part of the security improvements in Android 4.2 (JellyBean). Early third-party assessments of this feature have not been entirely positive, but it does provide some limited protection against users installing some existing malware accidentally.

[35] "State of Mobile Security 2012" report:

https://www.mylookout.com/resources/reports/state-of-mobile-security-2012

[36] Path uploads your entire iPhone address book to its servers:

http://mclov.in/2012/02/08/path-uploads-your-entire-address-book-to-their-servers.html

[37] Stealing your address book:

http://dcurt.is/stealing-your-address-book

[38] Vodafone privacy guidelines for developers:

http://developer.vodafone.com/develop-apps/privacy/

[39] Privacy design guidelines for mobile application development:

http://www.gsma.com/publicpolicy/privacy-design-guidelines-for-mobile-application-development/

[40] Google bouncer beaten at Black Hat 2012:

http://www.computerworlduk.com/in-depth/security/3372385/google-bouncer-beaten-at-black-hat-2012/

[41] Jon Oberheide's applications being killed by Google:

http://jon.oberheide.org/blog/2010/06/25/remote-kill-and-install-on-google-android/

[42] Exercising our remote application:

http://android-developers.blogspot.co.uk/2010/06/exercising-our-remote-application.html

[43] Google flips Android kill switch, destroys a batch of malicious apps:

http://www.engadget.com/2011/03/06/google-flips-android-kill-switch-destroys-a-batch-of-malicious/

[44] Symantec:

http://www.symantec.com/en/uk/mobile-security

[45] F-Secure:

http://www.f-secure.com/en/web/home_global/mobile-security

[46] iZettle:

https://www.izettle.com/gb/

[47] Malaysia car thieves steal finger:

http://news.bbc.co.uk/1/hi/world/asia-pacific/4396831.stm

[48] Torture for pin details:

http://www.guardian.co.uk/uk/2008/jul/05/knifecrime.ukcrime

www.ingramcontent.com/pod-product-compliance
Lightning Source LLC
Chambersburg PA
CBHW051211050326
40689CB00008B/1274